Mini-Handbook for Jackasses:

Communication &

Relationships

By Jennifer Arvin Furlong

JENNIFER ARVIN FURLONG

DEDICATION

For my husband, Greg. For two decades we've been taking turns playing the role of jackass in our relationship. With a considerable amount of honesty, a healthy amount of humor, and a lot of bribery, we somehow make it work. I love you more than you can ever know, despite the fact you're a flaming extrovert.

For my children, Nate and Sarah. You make me a better person. No, seriously. You soften my hard edges and remind me every day just how much I love being a mom. You taught me the value of listening and how to love unconditionally. You have both grown into amazing adults, despite my many shortcomings as a parent. I'm so proud of you both.

CONTENTS

PREFACE

The Rules:

1. You should know this isn't your typical self-help book. Although I'm an academic, it's not written using academicianese. (Yes, that's a word I just made up. It means, written by academics for academics; not intended for consumption by the average lay person.) In other words, you can read this and understand what in the hell it's saying.

2. I write like I talk, which is straightforward but not always grammatically correct. What can I say? I'm human.

3. Avoid the self-serving mode. Keep reading with an understanding this book is most likely about you. When I'm describing the communication habits of a jackass, keep yourself in mind, not everyone else. Know that *you* are most likely the problem when it comes to instances of miscommunication and arguments. In many ways, this is your self-help manual. Read it. Learn from it. Apply it.

4. Have a sense of humor. Read between the lines and inflect a lot (and I mean *a lot*) of sarcasm. Smile—even when you recognize I'm talking to you about you. But don't consider this a green light to keep laughing it off and continue being a jackass. Consider this a type of wake-up call but with giggles.

5. Read with the intent to improve your own communication habits, not everyone else's. I cannot emphasize this point enough. You cannot change or control how anyone else acts, behaves, or communicates. But you can control how *you* act, how *you* behave,

and how *you* communicate. Quit blaming others for your lack of communication prowess.

6. Recommend this book to others. After having said everything above, you're not the only one who communicates like a jackass. I'm pretty sure you already know this. Leave this book at the doctor's office. If you're a manager, make the minions read it for professional development. If you're a minion, leave it on your manager's desk in the middle of the night. Give it as a gift to your significant other. You may get slapped, but that's okay. You're providing a public service. Spread the word and the world will be a much better place. Seriously.

1 INTRODUCTION

Since the dawn of man and woman, our species has managed to evolve and improve upon how we communicate. This ability to communicate with one another through language and symbols is what has allowed us to climb to and stay at the top of the food chain. Without communication, we would not have been able to pass on the knowledge necessary for survival or teach the next generation how to hunt, how to gather, how to build homes, how to live as a civilized society, how to win wars. Without communication, we would not have found books introducing us to characters we love and those we love to hate. We would not have experienced adventures through classic literature, hope and loss through song, differing perspectives through poetry, celebrity gossip through social media. Yes, humankind owes its greatness to the art of communication.

I can't help but wonder if we've peaked.

The invention of technology has enabled us to spread information to the masses in an instant. No longer do we keep personal journals tucked away somewhere private and safe. Now, we document our daily lives online for the world to see. Whether or not we're honest about our daily lives is . . . ahem . . . a matter of perspective. Just take a look at your Facebook friends and think about how awesome their lives must be based on their updates. Definite jackass material. But then again, there might be others out there who make you cringe when you read their posts. We'll get to those jackasses a bit later.

My point is, as great as technology has been for globalization, has it been good for the interpersonal relationship? I'm not talking about how your distant cousins and nieces and nephews can now keep track of your life through status updates and uploaded pics and vice versa. I'm talking about the important interpersonal relationships. You remember those? The people who *matter*. The husband, the wife, the son, the daughter, the nuclear family. As technology expands its reach and our dependency continues to increase, our level of intimacy decreases. Don't believe me? Do you talk to your immediate family more through F2F[1] or through technology? That's what I thought. And therein lies the problem. We have forgotten how to be intimate. We have replaced the other humans in our lives with laptops and smartphones and tablets. Instead of getting the real version of others, we have learned to communicate with the screen version. The result? The dehumanization of . . . well, everyone. Thus, the rise of the jackasses.

But all isn't lost. This can be fixed! The key is to realize you have to fix yourself, not others. Be the example and set the standard. Demand

---

[1] F2F = face-to-face communication

dinnertime be technology-free family time. Insist when others are in a conversation with you, they not text or check email at the same time and you agree to do the same. Don't post remarks on social media you wouldn't be willing to say in person or pics you wouldn't want your grandma to see. And for goodness' sake, when you're sitting in a classroom waiting for class to begin, look up from your smartphone and make some eye contact, will ya?

DEFINING COMMUNICATION

Before we jump into the first lesson, I need to make sure we are speaking the same language.

How about you take a quick moment and write down, in your own words, the definition of *communication*. No cheating!

Communication
is:_____.

Very good! Now, were you honest? Did you peek down this page for some help or ask your smartphone for the definition? Let me make it easy for you.

Google[1] (2015) has multiple definitions, but this is at the top of the list: "the imparting or exchanging of information or news."

Wow. Well, it sounds simple. Give and take. Kinda like a recipe swap. Then, what's the problem? Why do we have so many arguments and misunderstandings? If it were this easy, nobody would ever sleep on the couch.

Merriam-Webster's[ii] online dictionary (2015) offers a more complete definition: "the act or process of using words, sounds, signs, or behaviors to express or exchange information or to express your ideas, thoughts, feelings, etc., to someone else."

Okay, so this is sounding a little better. At least this definition is taking into account there are many ways to send a message. We write. We talk. We mime. If we feel it's important, we will find a way to let someone else know it. If we don't agree with another person's point, we use our words to call them a name like "stupid," or we respond with a loud fart noise, or we YELL AT THEM BY TYPING IN ALL CAPS.

Let's take a look at one more definition. This one is from Encyclopaedia Britannica[iii] (2015): "the exchange of meanings between individuals through a common system of symbols."

I like the use of the word "common" here. This is an important distinction between the many definitions of communication. After all, it's hard to exchange information when we're speaking different languages or when we attach different meanings to different symbols. For example, sometimes we use our hands to indicate numbers while communicating in America. We hold the hand up with the index and middle fingers extended, palm facing outward or inward, to indicate the number two, as in "I'd like two shots of espresso in my coffee." Travel to England, on the other hand, and make the same gesture with your palm facing inward. You just told the other person to "%@$# off" or, in milder terms, said "up yours." Yes, it's very important to make sure you're operating under a common understanding of the symbols you use while communicating.

Here's my definition of communication in its basic form: "the process of creating a shared meaning."

Yep. That's it. Now, of course, we try to create this shared meaning by sending and receiving messages through multiple auditory and visual channels, but the end result is the same. At the end of the day, whatever visual symbols we use, whatever auditory sounds we use, we're using them to try to send a message so that the person on the other end can understand what we're trying to communicate. Thus, creating a *shared meaning*.

Communication involves people and symbols and interpretations. The bottom line is, we need to remember the message you send may not be the message received; therefore, we must take care to create a *shared* meaning. Regardless of the intent. Regardless of the medium. Regardless of verbal and visual symbols. If we want to be effective communicators, we have to make sure to remember this point. And in order to create a shared meaning, we have to remain *mindful* of the messages we send and how those messages might be interpreted. That *mindfulness* is the key. It's become apparent too many people have lost their ability to be mindful (assuming they had the ability in the first place). And too many of those people are in the process of raising an entire generation that doesn't even know the word "mindful" even exists. As a result, we have a society of people who think they're effective at communicating, but they're only effective at sending out a bunch of messages. And sending out messages without being mindful of their impact can be a dangerous thing. Unfortunately, instead of getting better at communicating, our society is getting better at showing just how many jackasses we have in the world today.

So take heed. The following chapters are intended to help you avoid being the jackass in your crowd—if you aren't already.

2 THE SELF-CENTERED JACKASS

"Get over yourself. It's not about you. It's about them."

~Professor Speech Lady

I spend a lot of time pondering about and researching how to develop better and more effective communication skills in and out of the classroom. I've talked with high school kids and corporate managers, friends as well as business colleagues, family members, and strangers. After all this time, I've noticed something interesting . . . and disturbing.

Let's face it, most people's idea of improving their own communication skills involves learning how to get *others* to listen and follow directions better and more often. Don't agree with me? Do any of these questions sound familiar?

"How do I get the board to adopt my proposal?"

"How do I get the school board to understand this 'new math' is a waste of time?"

"How do I get my boss to listen to my complaints?"

"How do I get my coworkers to listen to my ideas?"

"How do I get my wife to stop nagging me?"

"How do I get my husband to leave the toilet seat down?"

Are you seeing a trend?

No? We have a lot of work to do here.

Here are some more examples.

"How do I get my husband to give me more compliments?"

"How do I get my girlfriend to leave me alone during the game?"

"How do I get others to understand me better?"

Figured it out yet? Let me help you. And pay attention, because my message will be a subtle one.

Get over yourself!

There. I said it. You see, here's the true problem. Most people (e.g. jackasses) aren't interested in improving their own communication skills. I mean, they think they want to improve their communication skills, but what they want is compliance. It's true you see a lot of "I" statements above that give the perception of self-improvement, but keep reading. There's a whole lot of focus on creating change in the other person and not on the self. Many people make this mistake. They think they want to improve their own communication skills, but they just want to find a way to get what they want. If this is your mindset, I am sorry. You are a jackass.

Please don't get me wrong; we all need effective communication skills in order to be more successful in our business and personal relationships, but it's not all about how we can speak better, use more power poses, dress better for success, or make stronger eye contact. It's about how often we can shut our mouths and allow others the opportunity to express themselves.

Make you a little uncomfortable? Not the answer you were looking for? Looking for the quick, 5-step program to communication success (e.g. how to talk and get others to listen)? I'm sure you'll be able to find that drivel in some other lame-ass self-help book, but not this one. If you want to improve your communication skills, then keep reading. I dare you. No, I triple-double-dog dare you.

You see, putting others first is the primary key to being a good communicator.

Here's my advice. Quit worrying about the outward communication stuff for now. We know getting your point across is important, but if you want to get to the core of being a good communicator, you have to stop focusing on yourself and your needs and start focusing on others and their needs.

Do you still want to be a better communicator?

The question isn't rhetorical. Now you know this book isn't going to stroke your ego . . . . Now you know the way to improve your communication skills is by focusing on your own shortcomings rather than others . . . . Now you know good communication is about them and not you. Do you still want to be a better communicator?

If the answer is yes, start here.

First, start by understanding you do not know it all. You don't have all the answers. You don't know anything other than what others tell you. Seek out the perspectives of others. Appreciate the fact others' perceptions will help you improve your own understanding of the world around you. If you don't want to understand the world by inviting in others' points of view, then you don't want to be a better communicator. Period. End of story. You might as well put the book down now, because you're already a jackass, and there's probably no going back.

Allowing another person to speak does not mean you have less power in the relationship, or you concede defeat in the argument, or you agree with the other person's opinion. Understanding another person's point of view doesn't equal agreement or approval. You can still disagree. Hell, it's likely that you won't ever agree, depending on the topic, but if you try to focus on the other person and at least try to make room for a different point of view, you just might learn something new. Again, this isn't agreement or a concession; it's just understanding.

Taking this approach to communication is very difficult for most of us because it goes against the grain of what we've been taught since childhood. We've been brainwashed into thinking we're all the same. Our conditioning has been so subtle we don't even realize we're guilty of doing the same to the next generation. And on and on it goes.

Here's the deal. In order to improve your relationships and become better communicators, we have to unlearn one very shiny golden rule.

The Golden Rule Myth

Now you've hopefully dropped the ego baggage and can put the other person ahead of yourself while in conversation. Let's move on and get to the meat and potatoes of effective communication. The first lesson in improving communication skills and interpersonal relationships is to understand the number one rule for relationship management we were taught since we were crapping in our diapers is bogus. Well, it's not completely bogus, but it does fall just a bit short.

"The Golden Rule[iv]" is probably most well-known in Christian circles as the premier guideline for how to treat people. In reality, this maxim is shared amongst many major organized religions across the globe. That's right. It ain't just the Christians spreading it around. Just take a look at the collection of examples below provided by Humanity Healing International[v].

Ancient Egyptian: *"Do for one who may do for you, that you may cause him thus to do."~ The Tale of the Eloquent Peasant, 109 – 110 Translated by R.B. Parkinson. The original dates to 1640 BCE and may be the earliest version ever written.*

Bahá'í Faith: *"Ascribe not to any soul that which thou wouldst not have ascribed to thee, and say not that which thou doest not."~ Baha'u'llah*

Brahmanism: *"This is the sum of Dharma [duty]: Do naught unto others which would cause you pain if done to you."~ Mahabharata, 5:1517*

Buddhism: *"Hurt not others in ways that you yourself would find hurtful."~ Udana-Varga 5:18*

Christianity: *"And as ye would that men should do to you, do ye also to them likewise."~ Luke 6:31*

Confucianism: *"Do not do to others what you do not want them to do to you."~ Analects 15:23*

Hinduism: *"This is the sum of duty: do not do to others what would cause pain if done to you."~ Mahabharata 5:1517*

Humanism: *"Don't do things you wouldn't want to have done to you."~ British Humanist Society*

Islam: *"None of you [truly] believes until he wishes for his brother what he wishes for himself."~ Number 13 of Imam Al-Nawawi's Forty Hadiths*

Jainism: *"A man should wander about treating all creatures as he himself would be treated."~ Sutrakritanga 1.11.33*

Judaism: *"What is hateful to you, do not to your fellow man. This is the law: all the rest is commentary."~ Talmud, Shabbat 31a*

Native American Spirituality: *"All things are our relatives; what we do to everything, we do to ourselves. All is really One."~ Black Elk*

Roman Pagan Religion: *"The law imprinted on the hearts of all men is to love the members of society as themselves."*

Shinto: *"Be charitable to all beings, love is the representative of God."~ Ko-ji-ki Hachiman Kasuga*

Sikhism: *"Don't create enmity with anyone as God is within everyone."~ Guru Arjan Devji 259*

Sufism: *"The basis of Sufism is consideration of the hearts and feelings of others. If you haven't the will to gladden someone's heart, then at least beware lest you hurt someone's heart, for on our path, no sin exists but this."~ Dr. Javad Nurbakhsh, Master of the Nimatullahi Sufi Order*

Taoism: *"Regard your neighbor's gain as your own gain, and your neighbor's loss as your own loss."~ T'ai Shang Kan Ying P'ien*

Unitarian: *"We affirm and promote respect for the interdependent web of all existence of which we are a part."~ Unitarian principles*

Wiccan: *"And it harm no one, do what thou wilt."*

Yoruba: *"One going to take a pointed stick to pinch a baby bird should first try it on himself to feel how it hurts."*

Zoroastrianism: *"Whatever is disagreeable to yourself do not do unto others."~ Shayast-na-Shayast 13:29*

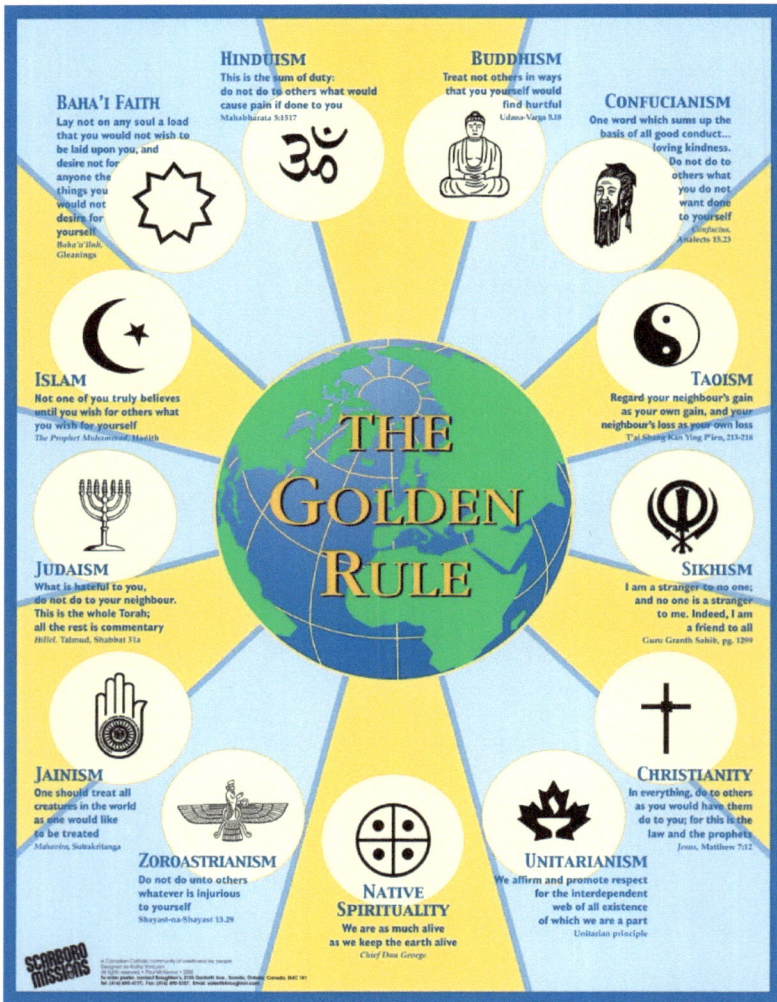

Figure 1 Used with permission from Scarboro Missions.

In many religions the Golden Rule is also known as the Ethic of Reciprocity, which says we should treat others the way we want to be treated. Basically, have some empathy and don't be a prick. Pretty sound advice, right?

At the surface, it is good advice. Most of us can relate to the importance of being kind and generous to others so they too will be kind and generous in return.

In a *very* informal one-question survey (and by informal, I mean my Facebook friends answered my question), I asked for respondents to explain in their own words what they thought the Golden Rule means.

Here are a few unedited responses. I left out last names to respect their privacy, but they know who they are.

Just like with the laws of physics ever action has a equal reaction. Give if you want to receive. Love if you want to be loved. Not many people realize everyone around you feeds off of your actions. Very rarely have I lost my temper and yelled or got smart with someone who reacted oppsitely. Means we need to take our time and think about how we want others to interact with us and use that as a template as to how to treat them. This also reminded me of a pagan saying. Do as you will as long as you harm none. — Brannon

Kudos to Brannon for pointing out how others feed off our actions. Too many people forget this important point. We do have choices in how we interact with others and those choices influence the world around us. Also, a big shout out for adding the pagan perspective!

It's what some would call being "politically correct," its what I call being respectful and mindful of others feelings and situations in any given situation. It means I want to be understood by you, so in turn I will make effort to understand you. — Nathanael

In his explanation Nathanael shows he understands the importance of modeling desired behavior and the value of remaining audience-centered. There is great value in reaching for understanding first.

To me, this "Golden Rule" means that in order to get your way in any of life's great adventures, then you must coerce others into believing that your intentions have them at center focus. This is that I believe that the unintended consequences of one's intentions become their reality. — Enrico

Although he has a slightly more cynical view and dances around the territory of manipulation, Enrico also points out the importance of remaining audience-centered. There is validity to being mindful of others needs and wants. If you keep the focus on the other person, they'll learn to do the same.

Doing to others as I would have them do to me, leaves peace of mind and no regrets, even if the doing isn't returned. Doing is self-satisfying. — Rose

In contrast, Rose has the more benevolent viewpoint. She's not worried about the return on investment. At least her conscience is clear.

Walk in love, be empathetic, forgive. — Linda

Short and sweet, Linda provides us with concrete instructions. Notice how she also didn't say anything about getting something in return.

There is a lack of kindness in the world today. When I was a child, I was taught to be kind and befriend all children that I came in contact with. Even if I couldn't befriend them, I was taught to "be nice". In our society today, I feel that there is a lack of kindness. People don't talk anymore. They stare at their smart phones and forget how to communicate and relate with each other. Relationships have taken a backseat. Do unto others means simply that....think about what you want from the universe and give that energy to it. — Adria

Adria is frustrated with the world. Can you blame her? Me too, girl! Me too! It feels as if kindness has left the world and smart phones have taken over our minds. She has a good point about where to focus your energy. Where is your energy focused?

If you slap someone, your a$$ is gonna get slapped back! — Mitchell

I knew I could count on Mitch to slap us back into reality. While most focus on being kind and respectful, he reminds us of the dark side of reciprocity.

To me, it's similar to 'you reap what you sow' meaning how you treat others is how they will treat you. — John

John reminds us to look in the mirror and take responsibility. If you're having trouble in a relationship, perhaps you should take a look at what you planted in your own backyard.

Golden rule. Is it really golden or is this a human trait that is so rare these days it's classified as golden. To many times we come across others that believe the opposite of this rule. Every once in a while you encounter believers of this rule and do not perceive it as golden but a personal standard of being a good human. Paying it forward would be the simple way to explain. – Mike

It sounds like Mike has lost faith in humanity. But the idea of paying it forward is one way to restore that faith. But this requires the same mindset as Rose and Linda. Don't expect anything in return.

"To me this means, simply, treat others the way you want to be treated." – Kat

"To me it means, treat people the way you want to be treated. So just be a decent human being to each other." – Brian

"Treat everyone with courtesy and respect and you will receive in kind." – Theresa

I think we have to teach people how to treat us. – Sondra

The Golden Rule is summed up nicely by the final few responses. Short and sweet, these responses are a great reminder of the control we do have over how others treat us. People can take advantage of you for only as long as you allow it.

These are all commonly held points of view where it concerns understanding the meaning behind the Golden Rule. All of these responses are perfectly valid responses, but I do want you to consider a better alternative where it concerns maintaining important, long-term relationships.

Although the Golden Rule is good advice for how to interact amongst other humans, it's not necessarily the best advice for the most important long-term relationships we have with significant others. The significant others I'm talking about are the spouses, boyfriends, girlfriends, friends who are boys, friends who are girls, family members, co-workers. The people with whom you spend most of your time and need to positive relationships in order stay happy and healthy. In this sense, the Golden Rule kinda stinks.

Here's a question I want you to ponder as you prepare your counterargument to explain why you think I'm crazy for thinking the-one-rule-to-rule-them-all is a load of pooh. If this popular rule has been around for so long and is preached across so many different cultures, then why isn't it working? People learn this rule all across the globe and are taught to adhere to it. Not everybody follows the rule, but I think most people at least *try* to follow it . . . for the most part. Call me an optimist. At the surface, it seems like a good rule to follow. So, if everybody knows this rule, understands its importance, and continues to propagate its teachings to our younglings, then why ain't it working?

I'll tell you why. Because the very basis of this rule, regardless of the good intentions, is flawed.

That's right. The Golden Rule is flawed. At least where your most important relationships are concerned.

It's flawed because it's still operating under the premise all people are the same. You are like me. I am like you. We are one. Cue the "Kumbaya" music.

I want you to take a look at all of humanity; look at our cultures, our desires, our looks, and our politics. We are NOT all the same. I am not like you. You aren't like your neighbor. We aren't all one. Scratch the "Kumbaya" music.

But Jen, surely you're mistaken. We all want the same things—peace, love, and understanding. Right?

Of course we all want peace, love, and understanding! But here's the thing: how we translate those desires isn't the same. What constitutes peace, love, and understanding to me will likely be very different from how you might define those concepts.

For me, having a peaceful relationship with my neighbors might mean I leave them alone. I give them their space. I might wave to them as I walk to the mailbox, but other than that, I pretty much leave them alone. For me, this is peace in large part because I am an introvert. I find it difficult to chitchat over subjects not important to me.

On the other hand, my neighbor might translate my peaceful actions as rude in that I ignore her. Perhaps she's the type to stop and have conversations with the neighbors when she sees them out working in the yard. Perhaps she views friendly, ongoing conversations with the neighbors as what constitutes peace. She might even view having the neighbors over for barbecues as a way to keep the peace. For her, this is peace because she is an extrovert.

According to the Golden Rule, I should treat others the way I want to be treated. Since my version of peace between neighbors is a wave and nothing more, that's what I'll continue to do. No chitchat for us. But it's all golden.

Not really, right? Because unfortunately, now I'm perceived by my friendly, talkative neighbor to be unfriendly and perhaps even rude.

Do you get where I'm coming from now? Let me break it down even further.

I'm going to treat you like I want to be treated; therefore . . .

Example 1: I'm uncomfortable with hugs; you won't be getting any.

Example 2: I don't like sharing emotions; don't expect to hear mine.

Example 3: I have little patience listening to others gripe about their problems; keep your mouth shut.

Example 4: My favorite flowers are daisies; therefore, I'll bring you some of those. I prefer dark chocolate, so that's what you'll get.

Do you see the fundamental flaw in the Golden Rule yet? It's passed from one generation to the next because humans need a way to teach people how to get along. How to have empathy for one another. But the examples above don't provide very much empathy, do they?

But how can this be, you ask? The answer is simple. Just take a look at the examples. All of them start with me thinking about me. It's all about me! And this is the fundamental flaw of the Golden Rule. To follow this rule means you are focused on yourself and your needs, not the other person. This is as far from empathy as one can get.

Gold is old and it's time to get with the times: Golden Rule 2.0. For short, we'll call this GR2.0. This version of the rule tells us to treat others the way *they* want to be treated. Hmmmm. But that would require me to pay attention to the other person and be aware of what makes them happy.

Yep.

GR2.0 requires you to think about the other person's needs and wants. It requires you to understand the relationship isn't all about you. It requires you to understand we're NOT all the same. We're different and that's okay. This, my friend, is what builds and maintains strong relationships.

Think about the different people in your life. Think about your relationships and how to apply GR2.0 to them, especially where it concerns communication.

For example, do you have a friend who prefers to talk on the phone versus texting? Perhaps she enjoys hearing your voice. Perhaps she feels talking on the phone is more personable and creates a stronger bond. You, on the other hand, are very busy. You don't have time to talk on the phone. You prefer to text a quick phrase or two just to check in. Rather than thinking about yourself, try the call. It doesn't have to be a marathon conversation. If you're too busy, you can let your friend know. "Hey, I only have a couple minutes, but I wanted to call and see how your day's going."

What if the opposite is true? Perhaps you have a friend who doesn't prefer to talk on the phone, but you absolutely love to talk on the phone. You know who you are. Just look at your phone records. You tend to max out allowable minutes every single month. Even if you feel the need to unload, perhaps a text to this friend asking if they have some time to talk would be better.

In either scenario, just imagine how good your friend would feel after you treat them the way they want to be treated, not the other way around.

Confession: I'm guilty of breaking the GR2.0 more than I care to admit. I'm an introvert. I struggle with the thought of picking up the phone just to chat.

I struggle with small talk. I'm telling you this to let you know you're not alone. I'm working hard to take my own advice. That's all any of us can do.

3 THE NON-LISTENING JACKASS

"The human animal is a terrible listener."

~Professor Speech Lady

The second step to improving your communication skills is to *focus* on the act of listening. No really, put down the damn smartphone and quit checking it every five seconds while someone is talking to you. Turn off the freaking TV and quit surfing the net while you're talking to someone over the phone. Trust me; you're not going to miss much, except for what the person in front of you or on the other end of the phone is telling you. You are engaged in a conversation with another human being. You say you want to be a better communicator, so prove it now. We are bombarded with distractions every second of the day. Being a good listener requires you to give your full attention, not just a part of it.

Listening is the most underrated communication skill we have. It's the part of communication we engage in more than any other, yet we still manage to ignore its importance. Everyone is so busy trying to figure out how to impress others through their outward communication, they've forgotten how important the skill of listening is. I blame social media. But that rant is for another time.

In order to improve this most valuable communication skill, you have to *want* to listen. None of this will work if you don't want to listen to the other person. I can hear the naysayers already. "But what if I really, really, really, really don't care about what they have to say?" Well, my question to you is, why in the world are you in a conversation with this person to begin with? Why even bother? Why don't you want to listen? What's the problem? Are you afraid of what they might say? Do you think your opinion is the only valid one? Have you "heard it all before?"

Just listening isn't good enough though. Did you know there are different *types of listening* you can use depending on the situation? It's true! Most communication scholars will break down the different types of listening into multiple styles. We've got empathic listening, critical listening, pseudo listening, comprehensive listening, appreciative listening, discriminative listening, and the list goes on and on and on. Reading about all of these different types of listening and trying to determine when and where to use them can be downright exhausting and confusing. I like to keep things simple, so we'll just break it down into two types for now—critical and empathic.

I'm focusing on just these two types of listening styles, because I believe at the basic human communication level, these two cause us the most trouble.

They're two different ways to listen; and yes, *you can listen wrong.* We've all used both listening styles in many different situations, whether we know it or not, but chances are we've used them incorrectly and at the wrong time. This is more likely true for the jackasses out there who don't think being mindful of listening is important.

Critical Listening

Critical listening is used to evaluate what a person is saying and to then draw a conclusion about the topic. You're analyzing the information so you can come back with an answer. You have to pay attention to what the other person is saying and ask yourself some questions: Is this information logical? Does it make sense? Does the information come from credible, unbiased, objective sources? This is very different from just waiting for your turn to talk. That's what a jackass does.

You also have to be aware of your own assumptions and prejudices. This means as other people are talking, you should avoid allowing trivial things—like how they look—to get in the way of your listening. When listening critically to another person, you need to pay attention to the message to make sense of it. This means ignore the mismatched outfit, or the worn-out shoes, or the rainbow of colors displayed throughout the hair, or the dialect. These are the very things that feed your basic assumptions about others and get in the way of listening.

Just because a person dresses a certain way, or talks a certain way, or has a certain skin color, or is a certain gender, or has a different lifestyle from your own, doesn't mean the message isn't valid. But you won't ever find out for sure if you allow those assumptions and prejudices to get in the way of listening to the message.

To improve your critical listening skills, you have to pay attention to the message and ignore the things that don't matter. Pay attention to the main points and the evidence used to support those main points. Remain objective and unemotional. Reserve those emotions to tap into the next type of listening I want you to practice.

Empathic Listening

Empathic listening is the exact opposite of critical listening and should be used when you're in a situation requiring you to provide emotional support.

For example, I know it's hard to believe, but not everybody wants you to solve their problems. As a matter of fact, it's pretty presumptuous of you to think you would have the answer anyway. If someone's griping about a problem, just shut up and listen. Let them vent. Haven't you ever just wanted to vent? And when they get to a point where they stop to take a breath, don't jump in and start babbling. Keep your mouth shut. They will take the nonverbal cue to talk some more. Remember, you aren't in critical listening mode here. You are in empathic listening mode and are only trying to provide emotional support.

If it's too much to keep your mouth shut, tell them you can see why they're upset (even if you can't understand it). Remember, your role as an empathic listener is to lend emotional support and NOTHING MORE. The moment you start asking questions like, "Have you tried this?" or "Have you done that?" is the moment you revert to critical listening mode and will be viewed as being the jackass. Just shut up and keep listening.

This doesn't mean you can mentally check out while the other person complains, cries, and whines. It's important to be present. Let them know you're listening with open ears by keeping strong eye contact and remaining mindful of their emotional state. It can be difficult, but try to put yourself in their shoes.

But what if you think they do want your help in solving their problem?

In that case, you should continue to listen and still *keep your mouth shut.*

Remember Chapter 1: this isn't about you; it's about them. If they ask you for your opinion, tread carefully. Instead of jumping right in and offering the solution, ask them questions like, "what do *you* think you should do about it? What have you already tried? What would you like to happen?" Continue to prompt them with questions, not answers. Don't think of yourself as the person who has the answer because guess what? You don't. Think of yourself as the person who can help them discover the answer for themselves. Some old story about the difference between giving a man a fish and teaching a man to fish comes to mind here.

When you learn to communicate *with* others, instead of *at* others, you'll begin to be viewed by others as a good communicator. And guess what? This is with you talking *less,* not more! This is with you asking questions, not making statements. When you've mastered this aspect of communication, then, and only then, will you be able to wield the influence you're so desperate to have. Otherwise, you'll just be the know-it-all jackass who gives bad advice.

Jackass Quiz – Listening Skills

If you've had a hard time practicing those critical and empathic listening skills, don't feel bad, because you're not alone. But if you're not quite sure about the level and quality of your own listening skills, keep reading to see how you measure up. Does the following sound like you? Dear God, I hope not.

Scenario 1

Assume everybody sees and experiences the world just like you do. You believe if they have a different opinion, they must be mistaken. You don't waste your valuable time listening to others' points of view to try to understand how they came to think or feel the way they do. It doesn't matter, because *your* perspective is the *right* perspective. As far as you're concerned, it's the *only* perspective. How can anyone else's experiences affect how they view and interpret the world around them? And does their opinion matter? Speaking of opinions . . . if another person dares to offer an opinion conflicting with your own, don't even bother to listen, because the experiences shaping how *you* view and interpret the world are the only legitimate and valid ones to take into consideration. All other opinions are invalid.

Let's just stop here and let all of that digest for a moment. You might want to read Scenario 1 again just for good measure.

Right about now you might be asking yourself, "What's wrong with having my own opinion and standing by it?"

There's nothing wrong with having an opinion. But do you realize it's an *opinion* and not *fact*? I know this may be shocking for some of you, but these two aren't the same thing. Let's start by taking a look at the latter concept first.

If I were to ask you to explain what a fact is in your own words, you might start with something like "anything that can be proven to be true." The reason I know this is because every single time I have this discussion in my classroom, students inevitably say this. Here's how the conversation goes (pretty much) every time.

Student: "A fact is anything that can be proven to be true."

Me: "How is it proven to be true?"

Student: "By research."

Me: "So if research says so then it's true; it's a fact?"

Student: "Yes."

Me: "Is chocolate good or bad for you?"

Silence

Student: "Good for you. Bad for you. It depends."

Me: "But I have research saying it's good for you, so according to you, since the research says so, it must be a fact. It's true. Chocolate is good for you, not bad for you."

Student: "There's research that shows it's bad for you too."

Me: "Okay. So are both facts?"

Silence

Me: "Yes? No?"

More silence

Me: "Then let's get back to the original question. What is a fact?"

Even more silence

Me: "A fact is anything that is indisputable. If the statement made can be disputed, can be argued, then it's not a fact. It's an inference. You must remember this when you make statements just as much as when you listen to others make statements."

The reason I offer this example is because it's important to understand we all have different opinions we like to think of as facts when, in reality, they are opinions. What may be true for you according to your beliefs or opinions may not be true for someone else. We arrive at our opinions based on our past experiences. Everyone's experiences are unique. Each of us has a journey of our own; therefore, everyone's perspective is unique.

This isn't to say you won't have people who share the same opinions. Of course you will. We meet people all the time with whom we can discuss various events and find we share similar opinions. What about the ones who disagree with us though? Because they disagree, are their points not valid? Remember, they're making their decisions based on the journey they've taken. On matters of opinion, their experiences are no less valid than our own. When you can begin seeing disagreements in this way and begin understanding the world is experienced through many viewpoints other than just one, your own perspective will broaden. You will find you're less prone to arguing and judging and more prone to listening for understanding and accepting the opinions of others.

Practice this and you just may make the transition from jackass to good listener.

Scenario 2

Multitask when communicating. Appease the other person talking to you by providing those feedback markers to fool the speaker into thinking you're paying attention. For example, just make sure you continue to nod in confirmation and say "uh-huh" every minute or so. This will help improve all your relationships—personal and professional alike. Not to mention it'll free up much needed brain space to think about other things. That's what you should be doing anyway when someone else is talking. After all, you're a busy person and can't be bothered with taking the time to focus on the person right in front of you or the person who's on the phone with you. As a matter of fact, you can partially listen to them while you think about and work on other things. It's easy. Just ask any married person.

As a matter of fact, just ask my husband.

I remember talking to the hubby on the phone while driving home from work one day. I had a horrible day. Anything that could have gone wrong did go wrong. The world was against me. So naturally, I'm giving the old man an earful, and he's giving me all the feedback signals.

"Yep. Uh-huh."

I go silent.

"That's cool."

"That's cool?" I said. "I'm telling you about my crappy day, and you say 'that's cool?'"

More silence.

Then, a chuckle.

"Oops. Sorry babe. I was focused on something else."

He's lucky I'm a patient woman.

Dearest Jackass, listen up. You might be able to get away with the multitasking while listening part of the time. You might even be so good at the fake listening you get away with it most of the time. But if you recognize yourself in any of these examples, it's time to stop being a jackass.

The ability to multitask is a myth. There is no human on earth who can work on multiple tasks simultaneously and do every one of them well. Think about it. As you try to do multiple things at the same time, what happens? It turns to crap. It's a hot mess. A soup sandwich.

For example, imagine you have multiple projects to complete. Under the theory of multitasking, you should be able to accomplish all of them at the same time. And you should be able to do an equally fantastic job on all of those different tasks. For those of you who've had multiple projects, you know this is impossible.

As a matter of fact, I struggle with this dilemma every single day. I'm struggling with this dilemma right now as I'm writing this very sentence. You see, at this moment I have laundry going, lunch warming in the oven, texts sounding off, and Facebook alerts popping up. I also have wallpaper to finish stripping in the master bathroom and new paint waiting in the master bedroom. I'm also shopping for a new bedroom suit. The power washer is calling my name because the back of the house is embarrassingly dirty. Donations (a result of spring cleaning) are waiting by the door to be taken away. Do you think I can get all of that done by multitasking? Hell to the no!

If I try to fool myself into thinking I can multitask and attempt to complete all of these projects at once, one of two things happens. Either I attempt to work on everything at the same time and I go insane, or I do a half-ass job at all of them and they never get completed. Something's gotta give!

The same holds true for listening. You cannot listen well unless you focus on the listening. This means if someone calls you, you need to look away from the TV or the computer. If you are physically in front of someone, don't check your text messages. If you are working on writing a book, leave the phone in the other room and don't even think about opening any other program besides the writing software you're using. That's a "note to self," by the way.

So the next time you find yourself nodding and giving the feedback cues just for the hell of it, recognize yourself for what you are—a jackass.

Scenario 3

React as emotionally as possible when someone says something you don't agree with or uses language you don't like. Listening for the meaning behind the message is an absolute waste of time. You shouldn't be blamed for becoming emotional and having a reaction whenever anyone says something you don't like or uses language that gives you heartburn. They should know not to use certain words around you anyway. They should know those words will trigger an emotional response. Your reaction is their fault, not yours. You shouldn't be responsible for your actions after that point. As soon as anyone says something you find irritating or offensive, immediately react with an emotional response. As a matter of fact, it's always a good idea to let them know you're listening by adding a physical response, like slapping them across the face or punching a hole in the wall. After all, the first reaction is the correct one, right? These types of responses will let them know you're listening *and* you're in complete control of yourself. Everyone knows the best decisions are made with emotional reactions, not careful listening and critical thinking. And anyone who thinks differently is a dumbass anyway.

Speaking of dumbasses . . .

If you think everybody else is the dumbass, then here's your wake-up call.

I'm not saying you shouldn't have passion when you communicate. Passion is good. Passion lets others know you care about the topic. Passion is much preferred over apathy. Try talking to an apathetic person and see what I mean. But irrational, emotional outbursts? Not so good. You see, there's a thing called emotional intelligence (EI). Ever heard of it? Basically it's the ability to not only recognize and be mindful of how you react emotionally in different situations, but to also be able to apply that knowledge in a positive and useful way. In other words, own your emotions. Don't blame others for how you react. When you take ownership of your emotions, take responsibility for your actions, you're emotionally intelligent.

There's been a lot of research over the years regarding EI, and some of it has managed to make its way into professional development sessions for business leaders across the land. I'm not going to knock it. I think everyone should learn more about this subject. It's just too bad we don't make the same type of development mandatory for the average human being beginning from day one.

It's not too late. You can still take responsibility now. Take control now. Don't tell me you're going to just accept you have no control and give the power over your emotions to others. This is too important. Don't be the emotional jackass at work. Don't be the emotional jackass at home. Raising your emotional intelligence level and owning your emotions and reactions could just be the answer to saving your relationship.

So this is where you take another good look at yourself. What are your emotional triggers? To whom or what have you given the power over your emotions? At the end of the day, you being an emotional jackass at work or at home is your choice. Do with this knowledge what you will.

Scenario 4

Listen literally. Take everything you hear at face value. After all, human beings are robotic creatures by nature anyway, right? There's no depth to them. There's no need to pay attention to stupid little things like intonation, eye contact, body posture, or facial expressions. Those are unimportant. As a personal rule, keep everything at the surface level and expect everybody else to do the same.

For example, ask your partner how he or she is doing. Regardless of the fact there's no eye contact, the shoulders are hunched, and the lips are quivering, the verbal response is, "I'm fine." You know you're in the clear and continue on your merry way. After all, anyone who says they're happy can be taken at face value. Why would anyone say something they don't mean? Don't worry about the shoulder shrug and lack of enthusiasm. Whatevs.

We all know if someone is unhappy or if they disagree with something you just said, they'd come right out and say so, right? Well, at least they should. Why should you have to pay attention to anything else other than what is being said? It's exhausting looking for and paying attention to nonverbal cues. If people would say what they mean – literally - relationships would work so much better.

If you've ever been the person (and you know who you are) who said, "Well, they told me they were okay, so I left it at that," then you've been guilty of being a jackass. Yes, you must consider all the messages being sent your way, verbal as well as nonverbal. In this instance, it's better to believe what you see than what you hear.

Scenario 5

Listen defensively. You know for a fact the vast majority of the time, when people are talking, they're talking about one topic: you. And they're usually doing so in a negative manner.

Paranoid much?

Of course you're not paranoid. You're not only a product of this negative universe, but you're at the center of it. Bad vibes revolve around you. It's not your fault. The world just sucks. People suck. People have told you you've got a chip on your shoulder, but they were just being jerks.

For example, last week your coworker asked if you're going to make the deadline. The nerve! He was obviously inferring you're incapable of getting your work done on time. What an ass. And you know damn well he wasn't going to offer to help out of kindness. Who does that?

And another thing . . . just the other day when your partner asked how long you're going to be out running errands or meeting up with friends, you know it wasn't because she was making plans for dinner or figuring out how much time she might have to run her own errands. Clearly it was because she was being nosy. She just wants to control you and your time. It was so obvious! Perceiving everything as a personal attack is the most helpful listening skill you've developed thus far. It does a great job of weeding out the people who are out to see you fail.

You know what? You're right about defensive listening being the most helpful listening skill. It is quite helpful . . . in showing the world how much of a jackass you can be. But don't worry about it. After all, the negativity is in everyone else's attitude, not your own.

People with this type of attitude are in need of more help than I can give in this one book. Unfortunately, I can't teach you how to have a good attitude. That's something you have to do for yourself. I'll tell you this, though. If you send out negativity to the universe, negativity is what you'll get back. If you send out positivity, positivity is what you'll get back.

Don't believe me? Try this experiment. The next time you go somewhere, be mindful of your facial expressions and body posture. What are you telling the barista about yourself as you're ordering your cup of coffee? Do your face and body say, "Hey! I'm a happy person, and I'm glad to meet you today!" or are you nonverbally screaming, "Hey! I'm an asshole, and I'm going to be your worst customer of the day because my attitude sucks!" In this experiment, go to different places and try both the positive expressions and the negative expressions and see which will get you a more positive reaction. I'm willing to bet your next paycheck the former will get you a lot further.

Attitude impacts perception as well as the world around you. Stay positive.

Scenario 6

Always jump to conclusions before the other person finishes talking. Hell, you already know what most people are going to say before they say it anyway. No one holds a surprise for you, especially if you've known them for some time.

You're also an excellent people reader. You can pretty much tell everything about a person just by looking at them. You can make an assessment of the other person and know how they feel and what they think about things. It's a true talent. Really.

As a matter of fact, you might have some psychic abilities. You just haven't been officially diagnosed . . . yet.

Understand this. You might be right about being able to read people 99 out of 100 times. But also understand this: there is always a chance you're wrong about what you think they may be thinking or what they'll say. If you can manage to keep your mind open and your mouth shut long enough, they just might surprise you.

Scenario 7

Always talk about the subject you know the most about. Yourself. You are the master at conversation rerouting. No matter what the other person talks about, you manage to jump in and relate a personal story. The central character of this story is, of course, you. Your stories are more exciting anyway. Plus, why not keep the focus on yourself? You are the most interesting person in the group.

Nothing can draw attention like the jackass who continues to make noise. Don't get me wrong here; there's nothing wrong with relating to a person's story. It's wonderful when we make a connection and find we've something in common or we've shared similar experiences. Sharing stories and understanding what we have in common is what builds relationships. But you might allow the other person to at least finish their story before jumping in and one-upping them.

Scenario 8

This scenario I'll start with a simple question. Do you really listen or do you just wait for your turn to talk? There is an important distinction. You might be the type of listener who allows the other person all the time in the world to say what he or she needs or wants to say. You sit there with strong eye contact and attentive head nods, but all the while, you're just rehearsing in your head what you're going to say when it's your turn to talk.

This, my friend, isn't effective listening. When the other person is done talking, you should be able to summarize what he or she said in your own words. If you can't, you weren't paying attention.

The lesson?

If you recognized yourself in any of these scenarios, you know what you have to do, jackass. Stop! Realize listening is so much more than just hearing someone else make noise and then responding with some noise of your own. If you want to improve your relationships, you're going to have to practice the listening stuff. You can do this in three simple steps.

1. ***Choose to focus***. As soon as you engage in a conversation, you have to tell yourself you're *choosing* to pay attention to the person who is

talking to you at this very moment. This isn't the time to multitask. This is the time to pay attention and take it all in. If you're having a F2F conversation, ignore everything else around you. Turn your body so that you're facing the person. Don't look around like you're looking for something more interesting to happen. If this conversation is taking place over the phone, get up from behind the computer. Get up from the couch and stop watching TV. You cannot focus on a conversation if you're too busy updating your status or catching up on the latest episode of your favorite show.

2. **_Mind the moment._** Be mindful of what type of listening the situation is calling for. Is this person just talking to you to vent, or is this person wanting you to help solve a problem, or is this person just wanting to chat for fun? It's important to make this determination, because you don't want to ruin the conversation by opening your mouth and saying the wrong thing. Sometimes people just need to complain, to pitch a little temper tantrum, and then they're fine. They leave the conversation feeling like you're the best communicator in the world when, in reality, you didn't say a word. But you listened.

3. **_Make it about them._** Remain engaged by asking questions. Lots of questions. One of my favorite quotes is from Larry King[vi], "I remind myself every morning: Nothing I say this day will teach me anything. So if I'm going to learn, I must do it by listening." Allow the other person to speak as long as he or she needs or wants to speak. As they are speaking, remember to hear between the lines. Listen for understanding. As you are listening to the words, pay attention to the nonverbal messages also. Everyone experiences and perceives the world differently. Imagine what you will learn when you listen.

4 THE SELF-SERVING JACKASS

"Don't point fingers unless you're willing to start with the mirror."

~Professor Speech Lady

When poor communication happens, it's easy for us humans to place the blame on others. It's natural. We are competitive creatures by nature, so when an argument ensues, of course it's the other person's fault. It's the jackass in all of us. In communication we call this the self-serving bias. Here's the theory: when something positive happens, we tend to attribute the success to our internal abilities—things within our control. When something negative happens, it's because of external factors—the things out of our control.

For example, I bet you think you got promoted because you worked so hard. You put in the time. You arrived to work early and left late. You volunteered for additional projects and always met the deadlines. Any time there was an opportunity for professional development or training, you were on board. The promotion was the reward for all you did for the company.

On the other hand, let's say you didn't get promoted. You'd feel quite different about things.

Perhaps the boss is biased, or the promotion process is unfair. You've seen the other person who got the promotion drinking with the boss after hours. You know they play golf together. As for all the work they've done— the meeting of deadlines, the volunteering for projects, the going back to school and going to training . . . What a kiss ass!

Here's another example. This is one I hear in the classroom. I hear students either brag about or complain about their grades throughout the semester. When students get a good grade, they'll say it was earned because of hard work and effort. They had to study sooooo hard, or they spent weeeeeeks on the research paper. No doubt the grade was earned.

Unfortunately, not all students get good grades. The students who get a bad grade will say the grade was due to unclear instructions or the unreasonable expectations of the instructor. If they had been given more time, they would have done better (despite the fact the assignment was listed on the syllabus the student received on the first day of class). Sometimes students will blame others outright for the poor grade. Their child got sick the previous night, which is why the paper was submitted late with errors. (My response? But you've had weeks to do this.)

In short, the self-serving bias explains just how far people will go to avoid taking responsibility for the negative things that happen to them. Promotions are earned, unless said promotion went to someone else. Good grades are earned; bad grades are given.

Unfortunately, the self-serving bias is also alive and well in our daily communication. Think back to some of the misunderstandings you've encountered over the past few months. Did you sit back, reflect, and conclude YOU could have—and should have—done something differently?

If you did, I'd be überimpressed. But I'm thinking it's likely you didn't. The misunderstanding was the other person's fault. As a matter of fact, misunderstandings are usually the other person's fault, right?

What can I say? The world is full of jackasses. I suggest you start watching your back. Surely someone is about to play Pin the Tail on the Donkey.

If you haven't noticed, the self-serving biased isn't too far from the victim mentality. You know that person (it could be you) who, no matter what, is always the target of an unfair world. They were born poor. Dealt a bad hand. Their dad was an alcoholic. They were raised by a single mom. The system is rigged and there's no way to get ahead. They always have an excuse as to why they either can't do something or why something went wrong. While they're busy feeling sorry for themselves and being a victim, others are running over, digging under, moving around, or tackling through roadblocks toward a better future.

So this is the third lesson in improving your communication skills. You need to rework those wires so the blame doesn't automatically default to someone or something else. After all, if you learn to take responsibility for your part in whatever happens, you'll learn you also have the ability to change the outcome for the better, regardless of your past and regardless of what the other person does.

Your past does not define you. The choices of others do not excuse or validate your personal choices. The behaviors of others do not dictate your own behavior.

For example, if you just received a less-than-desirable grade on a research paper, think about what you could have done differently to create a better outcome. Could you have started writing earlier? Could you have gone to the library more often? Could you have asked for help? I'm willing to bet the answer is yes. You just have to be brave enough to admit it and accept it.

This holds true for relationships too. Again, think back to some of the misunderstandings you've had in the past few months. Perhaps you had an argument you believe was the other person's fault. Now, stay with me here. This is going to be uncomfortable. Perhaps it'll even hurt. Don't entertain the thought of what the other person did to piss you off during the argument. Only think about the part you played in the fight. Pick at least one thing you did or said that could've been done or said differently to produce a better outcome.

For example, think about all the messages you were sending, both verbal and nonverbal. Were you shouting? Were you standing? Were you listening or engaged in some of the jackass types of listening discussed previously? Were you tired? Were your facial expressions controlled? Were you using expletives and calling the other person degrading names? I could go on and on. As you reflect on these questions, think about the impact it might have made if you had changed just one or two of these messages.

It's very tempting to revert to being an immature child and respond with, "Yeah, but he said this! She said that!" So, I'm going to explain it to you like I explain it to my own kids.

In every situation you find yourself, you have choices to make. Those choices will impact the situation in a positive or a negative way, regardless of what the other person does or says. You cannot control how the other person behaves. You cannot control how the other person thinks. You cannot control how the other person speaks. But you *can* control your own actions. Your own thoughts. Your own words.

Despite the other person, you must commit to taking responsibility for your part in the argument. If you commit to taking the situation in a more positive direction, there's no guarantee the other person will follow your lead. It won't be easy, but it's worth a try. Remember, we're dealing with human beings.

Communication isn't always easy.

5 THE SOCIAL MEDIA JACKASS

"The Internet is not an invisibility cloak."

~Professor Speech Lady

According to the Pew Research Center's[vii] Internet Project, as of January 2014, 74% of online adults use social networking sites. Of those adult users, 71% use Facebook. Facebook's[viii] July 2016 report stated it surpassed 1 billion (yes, that's billion with a "b") daily active users. Going back to the Internet Project, 23% of the online adult users use Twitter. Twitter[ix] reported on its website it has 313 million monthly active users. As for other social networking platforms, 26% use Instagram, 28% use Pinterest, and 28% use LinkedIn. That's a lot of people vying for attention. That's a lot of people showing they have the not-so-recessive jackass gene.

Unfortunately for all of us, this means we're nowhere close to having a shortage of jackasses. Just look online and you'll find a plethora of examples. Whether they're accidental or purposeful jackasses is debatable. Who knows if they mean what they've written online? Besides, not of that matters, because once you've acted like a jackass online, there's a permanent record of it.

Jackass Quiz – Online Communication Skills

If the actions below sound familiar, then it's time for you to learn and practice some online etiquette.

Scenario 1

You believe social media is the best way to update family and friends (and the general public) about the most intimate and personal events in your life.

Birth announcements, engagements, graduations, oh my! I know, I know. In today's day and age of technology, who isn't letting the world know about the birth of the newest member of the family or about Susie's high school graduation? It's a sign of the times. Let's face it; it's even expected. Family and friends flock to social media to witness these major life events. After all, sometimes it's just impossible to be at the actual event, so we reach for the next best thing in order to feel we're a part of that special moment.

These aren't the events about which I am speaking. I am speaking about those most intimate of announcements. Those comments that would normally make others cringe if mentioned out loud in a large gathering of "normal" people. Unfortunately, you may not even realize you're the person who does this. Have you ever been told you lack the all-important yield sign meant to be situated between your brain and your mouth? Perhaps you haven't had this problem in F2F situations, but somehow you feel freer to make others' jaws drop by posting wild comments online. When it comes to making people aware of major events, you need to understand the rules here. Depending on the event and the person, you may want to reconsider the medium through which you make the announcement.

Consider this…

What child wants to find out about their parents' divorce on Facebook or Twitter? What sister or brother wants to find out about a sibling's death? Who appreciates being dumped by their significant other online? What daughter relishes the thought of having her first menstrual cycle announced to the masses? Who wants to know about your bladder infection? You may or may not be shaking your head right about now, but this stuff happens. I've seen it. And I've wanted to gouge my eyeballs out afterward.

Some folks say we must embrace technology and make the most logical use of it. They believe relationships are somehow different because technology now rules the world. To those people I say, "no duh!" Of course technology has had a profound impact on relationships. I don't think anyone could argue the opposite. But just as with F2F communication—or any other type of communication, for that matter—certain rules still apply. If you believe delivering bad news in person is overrated and time consuming, we have some work to do, bub. And if you avoid giving bad news in person because it makes you uncomfortable and because you like to avoid conflict, that's a different self-help book (coming soon). Either way, technology isn't always the best way to deliver a message.

Memorize the following rule. Write it down and keep it on you in the event you forget.

The closer the relationship, the more personal the mode of

communication.

For example, let's say you're getting a divorce. Who're the people closest to you who'll be the most impacted by this life-changing event? If you have children, no matter how old they are, you better recognize they'll be affected. Definitely more so than friends and family you may see once in a blue moon. It's best giving this news in person to those who will indeed feel the ramifications of the divorce. If the kids are all grown and have already flown from the coop, a phone call is the next best thing if you can't deliver the news in person due to the distance. Trust me. This news matters to them, and how you decide to deliver this message says just as much as the message itself. If you don't heed this advice, don't be surprised if the kids don't take your side and you become the family mule.

If you're still confused or just aren't sure about the appropriateness of your announcement and the best mode of communication to use, refer to **Figure 1**.

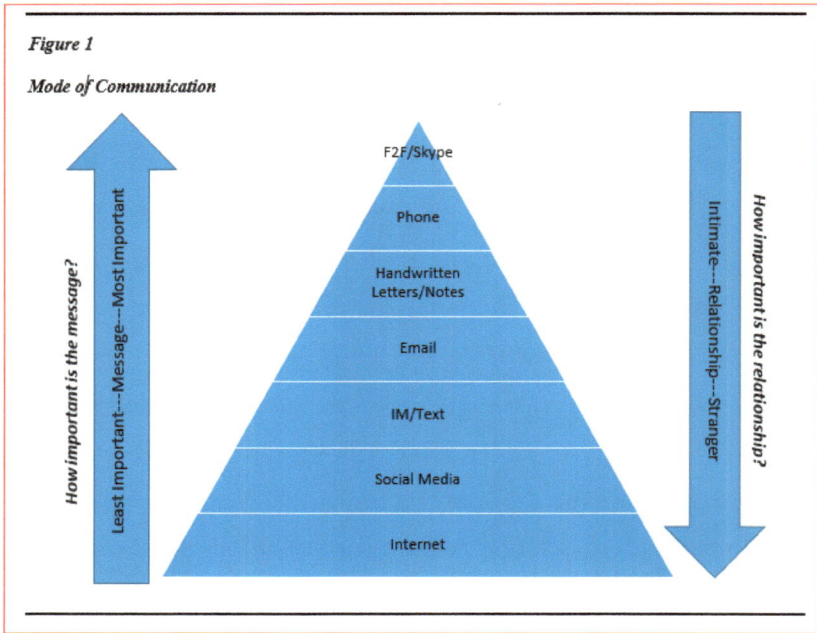

Figure 1

Mode of Communication

When considering the most appropriate mode of communication, there are several things to consider. First, consider the type of relationship you have with the recipient of the message. For example, do you have a close relationship with this person, or is this person more of an acquaintance? Additionally, consider the level of importance of the message. Is the message a funny meme about cats, or are you announcing you have cancer? The more intimate the relationship and the more important the message, the closer to the top of the pyramid you should be.

This isn't to say you should never communicate with your loved ones via social media. There are plenty of times it's appropriate, perhaps even preferred. Just consider the importance of the message. The number one way to establish yourself as a bona fide jackass is to let the most important people in your life know the most important information about you through the least intimate type of communication. Nothing says "you don't matter" or the topic doesn't matter like finding out funeral arrangements through a Twitter announcement. If you don't mind being looked at as a donkey, then go ahead and change your relationship status online without first having a conversation with your significant other. Better yet, just shoot them a text. That always goes over well.

If you're involved in an intimate relationship, and the more important message, the closer to F2F you should be.

Remember when you were little and you were told to watch your tone of voice? Boy, I do! The tone of my voice was apparently way off pretty much all the time. *How* you say something is just as important as *what* you say. In our age of technology, the mode of communication impacts the tone of the message. Just as body language and tone of voice can impact how the message and the messenger are perceived, so too can the mode of communication impact perception. You can't tell someone's tone if you're not speaking to them directly. It's much easier to misinterpret their intended tone or project your own twisted meaning into a text or status update.

Consider the recipient. Consider the mode. Consider the impact. Or just remain a jackass. Choices, choices.

Scenario 2

You enjoy playing games online and want all your friends to join you . . . or at least know your high score.

We like our online games, don't we? I know I do. Because I'm a nerd at heart, I love word games and strategy games. Others enjoy sports, or simulations, or casino games. Whatever your cup of tea, those games can be so exciting and fun! So, is it so wrong to want to spread the excitement and fun around?

Many jackasses don't think so. Go ahead and invite all your contacts to play the latest trend. Again. And again. And again. And don't limit yourself to just one. There are so many games to provide countless hours of online enjoyment. Your online friends don't mind getting the invite—from you as well as everyone else playing those same games. Continue to invite everyone to play, no matter how many times they ignore the invite or how many times they implore the masses via a status update to not send them game invites. Surely they don't mean it. And when you do continue to send out random game invites, they understand you're just trying to earn extra coins/points/whatever. After all, you're about to go up another level, dammit, and need their help to do so!

Oh, and don't forget to update your status every single time you go up a level or win a game. People are bound to be impressed by your gaming prowess.

If this sounds like you, the only level you'll keep moving up is from baby jackass to full-on adult jackass. Stop. Just stop.

Scenario 3

You believe what you say and do online is protected by the First Amendment.

The greatest thing about the Internet is the freedom it provides. The freedom to research what you want. The freedom to make connections with anyone and everyone. The freedom to show what you want. The freedom to say what you want. If your alternate personality has been waiting for the perfect moment to make an appearance, the Internet is the empty stage for its debut. Perhaps it's not even an alternate personality wanting to run wild and free in the online universe; this is your opportunity to show people who you are. Finally, you can take off the mask and not worry about being judged.

Your time on the Internet is exactly that—*your* time. Personal and professional relationships be damned. This is important, especially for those of you who either currently have a job or might be looking for a job one day.

Your posts are nobody's business but your own.

Go ahead and post inappropriate remarks and/or pictures all over your many social media accounts. You're an American, and it's your right to do so. You don't need to worry about little things like professional upward mobility and career stability do you? Who needs or even wants a good job anyway? Remember, *you have rights.* The First Amendment guarantees it. After all, you just want to make sure you look good to your friends. It's all for fun anyway. It's not anyone else's business.

Listen up. You may have First Amendment rights, but it doesn't mean there won't be consequences.

On Device Research[x] recently reported, "one in ten young people have been rejected for a job because of their social media profile." These job rejections were directly related to the comments or pictures posted on their online profiles!

And if you already have a job, don't think you're safe from being fired. Nothing could be further from the truth. There are countless examples of people who've been fired for their online activities. They were fired for a variety of things like badmouthing the boss, posting party pictures (and that's party pronounced with a *par-taaaay*), posting derogatory remarks about customers, etc.

The First Amendment does not give you an automatic get-out-of-jail-free card to say whatever you want in person or online. Think about it. What happens if you openly threaten to harm the president of the United States? You end up with your house surrounded by a bunch of people who look like extras off the set of *Men in Black*. You cannot say whatever you please or write whatever you want without repercussions.

If you were badmouthing or gossiping about the boss or other coworkers in person, to other people, and that information made its way back to the boss, you don't think there *might* be consequences? If you were to post naked pictures of yourself on the bulletin board at work, you don't think there *would* be consequences? Your actions online are no different from your actions in the "real" world. As a matter fact, it's best if you think of the online universe as another aspect of the "real" world. Hopefully, this attitude will help keep you out of trouble.

Scenario 4

You believe social media is a legitimate way to resolve conflict.

We all know and understand we can't be friends with everybody at all times. Sometimes we have disagreements. Sometimes our personalities clash. Sometimes we just can't get along. We. Are. Human.

You, however, believe in taking these interpersonal conflicts to the next level. Online. If you *really* don't like someone, you understand it's unhealthy to keep all that anger and hatred inside. And when you're pissed off at another individual, you know the value of resolving conflict in any way you can. And for you, it's no problem to let the world know about it.

Too bad you have a passive-aggressive nature. For you, letting another person know in person you have a problem with them is unthinkable. Normally, you'd just complain to yourself while not resolving anything, but now you have technology. Now you can post random, mysterious comments you know the other person will read. That'll learn 'em. Even better, when you've had it, nothing makes you feel better than letting the other person know it through your various social media platforms.

Regardless of how good this makes you feel, just know this feeling of accomplishment will be very short lived. Nothing good can come from airing the dirty laundry in an online public forum. As a matter of fact, posting while angry not only makes you look like a jackass, but now there's a permanent record of it.

Learn to resolve conflict in a more constructive manner. First, you must realize conflict is normal. Just because you disagree about a topic doesn't mean it's the end of the relationship . . . or the world. Second, you must realize you need to pick your battles. Not every disagreement is worth getting into a conflict over. Take a step back and look at this issue from multiple angles. In the grand scheme of things, is the fight even worth it? Sometimes, for the sake of the relationship and your sanity, it's better to let the other person have this one. Third, you must recognize ignoring the problem will not make it go away. Yes, we've all heard the saying time heals all wounds, but it doesn't apply to all situations. If you're the type of person who hopes to sweep the problem under the rug like you do the dirt in the living room, you'll soon discover, just like the dirt in the living room, it will eventually become too much to hide. At some point it will overflow and be an even bigger mess than it would have been if you'd just cleaned it up the right way the first time. Unfortunately, this doesn't include resolving conflict over social media. And posting mysterious or smart-ass comments online does nothing to help your cause. Don't be a pansy and hide behind your keyboard. Nobody likes a pansy. Especially a pansy jackass.

Scenario 5

You believe social media is the perfect platform for ranting.

You aren't afraid to share your opinions, no matter how close-minded and opinionated they make you appear . . . especially where it concerns politics and religion. These are two areas where you should have the last say, and you normally do because you are always right. Besides, anyone who disagrees with you (especially on your own wall) is the one who is close-minded. You aren't the one who should be expected to tolerate different opinions or ideas. After all, if anyone has a different point of view, they can share it on their own page. If you don't like it, you won't read it.

Posting your opinion once isn't enough. You must saturate the audience with your knowledge of the world. It's your duty to share wisdom ad nauseam. And don't worry when others unfriend you or stop following you. That's their problem, not yours. Who cares if it begins to look like you have no life outside of politics and religion?

Moreover, it's useful to use as many demeaning labels as possible to identify the groups of people you think are always in the wrong. Everyone knows if you belong to a group you all think alike anyway. That's why *you're* in a group—to have your ideas reinforced by like-minded individuals. Learning about different perspectives is useless.

Name calling online is helpful. Refer to Republicans as Rethuglicans. Refer to Democrats as Commiecrats. Show the utmost intolerance of other religions, and let everyone know they aren't going to heaven unless they believe in the same thing you do. If you can't convert them, no one can.

Now don't get me wrong when I say this, but if the description above sounds a bit like you, you have got to get a life! Other than the life of a jackass. It's great to be involved in the democratic process. I believe if more Americans would get involved and pay attention to the issues, we as a nation might stand a chance to remain a world superpower. But your life cannot always revolve around politics and religion 24/7. Don't you like to do anything else? Do you read? Do you run? Do you go to the beach? Do you paint? Do you dance? Do you sew? Do you play games? Sports? Music? Anything?

The silence is almost deafening.

It's just not healthy to be 100% consumed by argument and negativity all the time, and if you're only concerned with religion and politics, I'm willing to bet you feel stressed out a lot of the time. You might say you're not stressed because you enjoy discussing religion and politics. I challenge you to expand your experiences. You might not even realize how much better life can be until you move away from the keyboard and the TV and become involved.

Get out and enjoy your life (we only get one we know of). I'm not saying to give up on being involved in politics or spreading the word of your god(s), but for Pete's sake, get a life!

Scenario 6

You believe the masses need an update on your bladder infection.

For you, there's no such thing as TMI. You're just being honest. And is there anything wrong with asking for prayers and good thoughts? Okay, so maybe sometimes you need to let people know just how much you're suffering, is that so wrong? Who doesn't need a shoulder to lean on every once in a while? The shoulder you lean on for strength just happens to be social media.

This is why you don't think there's anything wrong with posting your most intimate, personal, and private information. But you don't stop there. You also make sure to post family members' most intimate, personal, and private information. You know for a fact everyone needs an update on the rash of illnesses you've been going through, like the high blood pressure and kidney infection. And your daughter will not mind at all you just announced to the world she started her period. She may even thank you for it once she sees how many prayers and good thoughts will be sent her way once everyone realizes her plight.

Hold up, jackass. Don't get your hopes up just yet.

It's more likely she will find a heavy object and hit you with it. Hard.

There are two issues to discuss here. First, why in the world would you feel the need to update the world on your bout of gout? Is it an attention thing? Be honest with yourself now. Perhaps I'm the one who's too private, but I cringe at the idea of asking my friends and family to keep me in their prayers as I battle a yeast infection.

Ewwww is right!

Look, it's one thing to want the strength and support of friends and family around you when you've been in an accident or are fighting a serious battle (like cancer), but it's a different thing to update friends and family on your latest battle with foot fungus. Trust me when I say this: nobody, and I mean *nobody,* needs or wants to know.

Lastly, double check with the person first before announcing they are in the hospital. Maybe, just maybe, they don't want the world knowing their business. It should be their decision to make their medical condition public, not yours.

Scenario 7

You believe you'll look cool when you announce the bad things you did today.

Go ahead and skip school and/or work and brag about it. Ferris Bueller might be able to get away with it, but you won't. Nobody's going to be wearing "Save (fill-in-your-name)" T-shirts around your school.

Okay, so you might be able to get away with it a time or two, but don't be surprised when the guillotine falls and it's your head in the basket. I'm not going to spend a whole lot of time explaining this one, because skipping out on school or work and bragging about it on social media is just plain stupid. Think about it this way: would you play hooky and then show up the next day and brag about it to your principal or boss?

Go ahead and try it, and let me know how it works out for ya.

And the same goes for breaking the law. Try posting a video of you driving 100 mph down I-95 or pictures of you robbing the neighbor or siphoning gas from a police car. Yes, that last one happened. I can't make this stuff up. That's not just being a jackass. That's taking the jackassness to another level of stupidity.

Scenario 8

You believe your social media contacts are just as excited about your latest "get rich quick" business venture as you are.

You've invested in this amazing online business opportunity. And you believe in the product! The catch? You need to recruit more people in order for this business opportunity to be successful. You already network with your friends via social media anyway, so why not make some money at the same time? You've so many online friends; there's no way you can't make money. It's like free advertising!

You're excited about your new venture and everyone else should be too. So you remind them to join your business several times a day, just in case they didn't see the previous invitations.

Now, don't get me wrong here. I'm not talking about the entrepreneur who has a legitimate product or service to sell. You could be crafty and good at making unique pieces of jewelry, or flower arrangements, or hair bows for babies. Perhaps you're a photographer and own your own business or an artist with a studio. Clearly, you are the business owner focused on selling products or services you created. It's genuine. It's unique. It's you.

I'm talking about the person who has gotten caught up in the latest pyramid scheme, aka multi-level marketing. Nothing makes you look like a jackass quicker than cramming your products down your contacts' throats every day, multiple times a day. Trust me on this.

Look, I know all about the value of using social media to network. As a matter of fact, I rely on Twitter and Facebook to generate clicks to my website. When I write a new article or have a clever quip to share, I'll post it on several sites. Hopefully, those interested in reading my drivel will visit my webpage. And if I'm lucky, those visits will result in someone booking me for a coaching session or speaking gig. Even better, perhaps they'll buy my book!

But I don't repeatedly ask people to visit my site. Every day. Multiple times a day. And I sure as hell don't market my services in the middle of someone else's posts.

Yes, this happens! I've seen it!

If you're involved in an online business and noticed you've gotten little response to your multiple daily posts—perhaps you've even been unfriended or unfollowed by a few people—make sure you're not doing any of the following:

When a friend of a friend posts pictures of their newborn baby, don't misinterpret the situation to be an advertising opportunity and post a comment about all the weight loss products they might want to buy from you. This is the action of a rude jackass. The same goes for announcing your most recent sale on cookware to someone's site when they're posting about the recent move into a new house. This is the action of a stalker jackass. Bringing up your business deals on another person's social media site is no different from those annoying calls you get from telemarketers in the middle of dinner.

Don't post comments like, "I recently found a REAL legit way to earn an income online from my own damn computer; how much better can it get? No I'm not FILTHY rich but I AM making money, and it's FREE to join!" on another person's page. That was a real post I saw one time, by the way. This is the clueless jackass. Do you think the owner of the page won't mind? Or the followers, for that matter?

Don't use your *personal* social media sites to make more announcements about your products and services than about your personal life. This is the unprofessional jackass. If you want to be viewed as a business professional, you need to create a business profile. Of course it's good to let your friends and family know about what's going on with your business, but allow them to follow your business page for those updates. Don't put your loved ones in the position of causing a family feud because they unfriended you or unfollowed your posts to avoid the endless stream of infomercials.

If, after reading this section, you find you're not a member of the social media club de jackass, congratulations to you! You've managed to make smart decisions where it concerns your online persona. I encourage you to continue making smart decisions to help you avoid personal and/or professional humiliation.

6 THE FREEDOM-OF-SPEECH JACKASS

"Just because you can say it doesn't mean you should say
it."

~Professor Speech Lady

Hey, this is 'Merica, and I can say what I want to! And if you don't like what I say, that's your problem!

Oh boy. If this is your attitude, we still have a lot of work to do . . . and I mean a LOT.

First, I'll refer you back to Chapter One for a review. If you've learned anything at all by now, I hope its understanding whatever you say is not their problem. It is 100 percent your problem, and this is why.

I'm going to first address this from a legal standpoint and then from a social responsibility standpoint.

Free Speech and Legalities
Amendment I **xi**

"Congress shall make no law respecting an establishment of religion, or prohibiting the free exercise thereof; or abridging the freedom of speech, or of the press; or the right of the people peaceably to assemble, and to petition the Government for a redress of grievances." ~ U.S. National Archives and Records Administration

This means the First Amendment guarantees certain freedoms regarding your right to practice any religion you choose or no religion at all. Also, it guarantees your right to express yourself freely, to assemble in groups, and to directly request an answer from the government if you're pissed.

This little handbook is about communication, so let's focus on the expression part.

Now, let me take a moment here to clarify something. I am not a lawyer. I am not here to offer legal advice regarding speech. I am writing as a communication academic and practitioner. Everything I write comes from either my own personal experience practicing in the field of communication or from research. So, if you find yourself in legal trouble for spouting off at the mouth, do not contact me. I repeat, do NOT contact me. Get a lawyer.

Moving on. As Americans, we understand the importance of our freedom of expression. This fundamental right stands at the very core of our ability to maintain a government for the people. There can be no democracy without a free press or without citizens who can practice freedom of thought and expression; however, just how far does freedom extend? At what point does the freedom of expression stop being an aid to democracy and start being an aid to destruction?

To answer this question, let's go to court. According to the Administrative Office of the U.S. Courts[xii], the following speech acts (whether words or actions) are protected by the First Amendment. We have the right

To not speak (as in reciting the Pledge of Allegiance or incriminating ourselves in court).

To use certain offensive words and phrases to convey political messages (what is considered offensive is debatable, though).

To advertise commercial products and professional services (some restrictions do apply).

To criticize public officials and public policies (criticize does not mean threaten).

To express ourselves online, except for obscenity. (It has been determined obscenity is of no value to society. Interestingly enough, pornography, however, can be protected as sexual expression for adults).

These guidelines don't change once we change our mode of communication to technology. Even in cyberspace, the same rules apply. First Amendment principles are being applied to blogs and Web sites and courts are considering social media like Twitter and Facebook to be protected under the free press clause.

You may not agree with some of these rights, but this is what freedom of speech and living in a democracy is all about. We cannot have a government of the people and for the people if the government reserves the right to force its people to behave and speak in a certain manner.

The First Amendment does not protect everything speech-related. There are legal limits to what we can say and do. For example, we do not have the right

To incite actions that would harm others like shouting "Bomb!" or

"Gun!" in a crowded building.

To make an obscene speech or to advocate illegal drug use at a school-sponsored event.

To make a "true" threat.

To commit treason.

To use "fighting words" (personally abusive language) . . . *more on this later*!

Admittedly, there is a lot of gray area concerning freedom of expression.

Another topic creating confusion and emotional distress is the question of prayer in public schools. The Supreme Court deemed school-sponsored prayer to be illegal because The First Amendment states the government may not establish any particular religion, meaning no endorsements of any religious faiths are allowed. However, students are free to pray alone or in groups, as long as school officials aren't involved.

Just as controversial is the recitation of the Pledge of Allegiance in public schools. According to The Newseum Institute[xiii], a nonprofit educational organization, two major issues are at the forefront. "1) whether students can be compelled to recite the pledge without infringing on their First Amendment rights and 2) whether the inclusion of the phrase 'under God' –

Pledge of Allegiance, by Dorothea Lange, 1942

added in 1954 – violates the establishment [of religion] clause." The former has been settled. Students cannot be forced to recite the Pledge nor can they be punished for opting out. The establishment clause is still in debate.

The original Pledge, proposed in 1892, stated, "I pledge allegiance to my Flag and the Republic for which it stands: one Nation indivisible, with Liberty and Justice for all." The phrase "under God" was added in 1954 by President Eisenhower. Because the First Amendment prohibits the establishment of religion, many Americans believe the "under God" phrase violates the First Amendment directly. Others argue it is ceremonial and not coercive; therefore, it doesn't violate the First Amendment. Clearly, this will continue to be up for debate for quite some time.

For some speech acts, the line between what is considered legal versus illegal is crystal clear. For others, the line will probably remain blurred for all eternity, but the Supreme Court can worry about that.

So we understand we have our First Amendments rights. We do have the *right* to say many things, whether they be positive or negative, but *should* we say those things? Although the government may not be able to (completely) censor our speech, there are times we should do so ourselves.

Free Speech and Social Responsibility

Remember this saying? "If you don't have anything nice to say, don't say anything at all." Well, that's the cleaned up version. Some of us remember it this way: "If you don't have anything nice to say, keep your f***ing mouth shut." There's an irony to that particular phrasing, isn't there?

One of the most perplexing aspects of free speech concerns the use of what could be considered (by some) to be foul or offensive language. According to the First Amendment Center, "fighting words[xiv]" aren't protected speech; however, how do we determine a "fighting word" from other uses of language one may just not like?

Whether you're cursing out a cop, or making insulting phone calls, or shouting profane language in a public venue, one thing is certain: behavior like this is likely to draw a lot of negative attention, but it's not necessarily illegal. The use of hate speech and vulgar language doesn't have to be mandated as illegal. Let me explain.

An individual's right to freedom of speech far outweighs an individual's comfort level regarding bad or offensive language. Using certain language and making certain hand gestures may be considered rude, but it doesn't make it a crime. But just because it's not a crime doesn't mean you should go all out and f-bomb the entire world with vulgar language.

Society has other ways of correcting those who have foul mouths and use less than desirable nonverbal signals. This is because, at its core, society understands language matters.

The words we choose to use every day matter. Language isn't just a reflection of reality; it helps create reality. Although they're intangible, words have powerful, sometimes life-changing impact. They can lift the spirit or crush the soul. They can create a bridge or cause a divide in relationships. Words are mighty things indeed. Don't believe me? Walk into any restaurant and yell (any derogatory term of your choosing) at another person and see what happens. As the kids say, "it's about to get real."

Because the words we speak can have such impact, we must be mindful of their purpose. We need to think before we speak and remember just because we can say something doesn't mean we should.

Let's be honest here. Sticks and stones can break our bones, and words can *definitely* harm us.

You see, we (you and I and every other egocentric human being out there) are such reactionary creatures. It's in our DNA. Whenever you hear something negative, I'm willing to bet it makes you feel pretty bad. With so much negativity in the world today, we humans tend to react in a negative way. Being creatures of habit, we don't even recognize we have negative responses anymore. We feel we're justified in our actions. We don't even recognize we're generating even more negativity continuing to encourage even more negative responses from others.

You might be thinking, "What can I say? The world is full of jackasses, so I might as well be one too." It's a vicious cycle. And it's destructive. It has to stop somewhere, so why not stop it now? Why not start with you?

Instead of spewing something offensive and negative out into the world, why not try something new, like saying something helpful and positive instead? In the heat of the moment, just ask yourself, "What can I say at this point to steer the conversation in a more constructive and positive direction?"

And by asking yourself this one question, you're practicing the art of mindfulness in communication. You're creating a better reality.

Now's a good time to address the concept of political correctness, because I'm certain some of you are already confusing it with what I'm talking about here. You're wrong.

For the critics out there, mindfulness in communication isn't the same thing as political correctness or PC. Too many people have confused cruelty with honesty. Crassness with freedom. Censorship with niceness. And too many people believe being mindful of the language you use equates to being PC. Nothing could be further from the truth.

You see, the idea of political correctness has taken on a negative connotation in our society. We value our freedom of expression so much we've warped the idea of being honest into the belief honest language is synonymous with offensive, and oftentimes cruel, language. Believe it or not, there are ways to express your honest opinion without using demeaning or derogatory language.

So, let's say you continue to use language perceived by others as offensive.

At worst, it could cause a physical fight. At best, it could cause others to view you as a bigot or a racist. Or perhaps others may just view you as a jackass.

Unfortunately, being perceived as a jackass or a bigot due to your inability to effectively communicate can have much larger implications than just an embarrassing moment. It can lead to strained friendships, broken workplace relationships, or being fired. And if you're a celebrity, be ready for the very public smear campaign by those you offended most.

At the end of the day, remember language isn't neutral. Communication is a catalyst to change. Whether the change is a positive or a negative one is 100 percent dependent on whether you choose to use language to build relationships and promote harmony or language to destroy relationships and promote suffering.

This doesn't mean you should avoid delivering bad or painful news. The way we deliver such news can be the difference between making the wound fester or helping the wound heal.

It's possible to be honest and compassionate at the same time. It's possible to deliver bad news in a way that can hurt just a little less. It's possible to disagree with a person's opinions without verbally attacking them. It's possible to have a debate without abusive and hurtful language.

Learning to use language in a constructive and positive way isn't only good for your personal well-being. It's good nourishment for others around you as well.

Research has shown our self-identity is influenced by how we believe others perceive us. We have a need to belong. To be accepted. This is why we join book clubs, play Xbox Live, rush for fraternities and sororities, and connect with others online. We seek out relationships for helpful and positive experiences. The last thing we want or need is to be with people who make us feel bad about ourselves. If we listen to negative comments enough (especially if those negative comments are about us), those comments will eventually affect us. In short, if enough people tell me I'm a loser, I might start believing it.

This is why it's important we practice mindful communication, including the language we choose to use. We can choose to use language to nourish or to poison. When you begin to understand what a powerful tool language is, you'll understand why we must use it responsibly.

7 THE SOCIAL-MORON JACKASS

"Nothing bad ever comes from being respectful."

~Professor Speech Lady

Please.
Thank you.
You're welcome.

A Facebook friend posted she wasn't going to "force" her daughter to say please and thank you to others. After spitting my coffee all over my iPhone, I wiped the screen as clean as possible with my t-shirt to make sure I had read the comment correctly. Perhaps I rushed too quickly while skimming over updates and read it wrong. It happens.

To my dismay, I did indeed read it correctly. She actually wrote she wasn't going to force her daughter to say the words please and thank you! It's almost like she wants her daughter to grow up to be a jackass.

When I first started writing this book, it didn't occur to me a chapter on basic manners would be necessary; however, humans never fail to disappoint. Many of them are what my husband calls "social morons." It didn't take long for me to realize this chapter absolutely is necessary. We need to get back to the basics. Well, at least the jackasses do.

Please.

This basic word is taught in our American culture to children starting as soon as they are able to talk and ask for things. Goodness knows little kids ask for a lot. They want the ball. The spoon. The toy. The cat's tail. A bite of your food. The list goes on forever. And how do we adults ensure that these little tikes understand the difference between a request and a demand? We teach those little buggers to say please. Seems logical. Seems reasonable to expect a young person to understand how to respectfully ask for something. Saying please is the way to do that very thing.

Just think about the difference between a request and a demand. The former shows you have an appreciation for the thing you want (and perhaps an appreciation for the person you're addressing), while the latter shows you to be a brat who thinks everything within eyesight belongs to you anyway and the people around you are mere minions there to do your bidding.

Furthermore, as we get older, it's important we understand we can't get through this thing we call life alone. We're going to need assistance along the way. Whether it's handing us a tangible object or getting someone to help us complete a chore at home or a project at work, saying please increases the likelihood of you getting what you want and shows the world you're not a jackass.

Thank you.

Just like the word, please, the phrase, thank you, is taught to our children from an early age. In our society, this is how we show gratitude for the things others do for us. It shows we recognize that person had a *choice* and we appreciate they chose to do something nice.

It's very simple, really.

If someone gives you a gift, say, "thank you."

If someone gives you a compliment, say, "thank you."

If someone gives up their seat for you, say, "thank you."

If someone holds the door open, say, "thank you."

Now, let me stop here and clarify something about the door holding thing. There are some, for whatever reasons unknown to me, who believe the act of holding the door open for someone else (specifically, a man holding a door open for a woman), is somehow demeaning to that person. Let's not get things twisted. Lady jackasses, I'm talking to you. If a man holds a door open for you, it doesn't necessarily mean he thinks you aren't capable of opening the door yourself. For example, my most wonderfully awesome husband holds the door open for me all the time. When we walk into a building, he opens the door for me. When we walk to our car, he opens the door for me. After 20-plus years of putting up with my crap, he still remains a gentleman. He knows I can open up the damn door myself. He just chooses to open them for me because he's a nice guy. They do exist.

I don't want to focus only on the ladies. Men, you have your fair share of jackasses out there as well. If another man or a woman holds the door open for you, say thank you. The person holding the door is not doing you a disservice. Don't be a jackass. Just say thank you.

And to my fellow door holders out there, like you, I too have held the door open for others only to feel the sting of rudeness from those who refused to thank me for holding said door. Just continue opening those doors. If they fail to recognize your generosity with a polite thank you, then just follow up with a resounding you're welcome.

Let's segue.

You're welcome.

No problem. Don't mention it. It's nothing. Sure thing. My pleasure. Glad to do it. No worries. Anytime.

Depending on where you're from, there are many ways to respond to a thank you. There are debates regarding the validity of each phrase, but whatever. If I tell you thank you, I'll be happy just to get any of these phrases in return. Unfortunately, all too often, jackasses forget the importance of uttering these replies.

Why does it even matter?

Saying you're welcome to someone who says thank you shows you acknowledge their appreciation and you understand their gratitude. A little recognition goes a long way with people. Somewhere along the line, we've forgotten this. Is it too much to ask for some follow through?

When you don't respond with some type of acknowledgement, it's the equivalent to ignoring that person. They were polite enough to say thank you, and you were jackass enough to ignore them. Good job.

So, where do we go from here?

Saying please, thank you, and you're welcome should not be words that come to mind only when something special happens. Having good manners is a matter of habit. And how do we create a habit? By doing the same action over and over again until it becomes second nature. In order to make good manners a habit, it's our job as adults to force children to say please, thank you, and you're welcome for it to stick. It's also important that adults model these behaviors for children to hear and see.

These are words that should flow effortlessly and honestly from the mouth to show that they stem from an empathic being with a good heart. These habits will help them be more successful in life.

Being polite out of habit shows we play well with others. That we're not an asshole.

These words show we value those who are around us and respect them.

Being respectful is something that should be a part of our being; not something that shows up every once in a while during random moments of kindness. And respect should not be something that goes away just because someone else lacks it.

In the past, our script used to be, "To get respect, you have to give respect." We taught our children to be respectful first, and then the respect will come back. Now it seems the other way around. All too often I hear people say, "If you want me to respect you, you better first give me respect." Excuse me, but this is completely jackass-backwards. Am I the only one who has witnessed this change for the worse?

Being respectful is a reflection of your character, not theirs. All of us will have the unpleasant experience of meeting many jackasses throughout our lives. These jackasses will not have manners. They won't be respectful. This is because they are jackasses. Don't you be one too.

The bottom line is, teach your children to say please, thank you, and you're welcome. You will be doing them a huge favor by doing so. Not only will they reap the benefits of being polite members of society, but the people around them might actually like being around them.

A side note about holiday greetings

Surprise! Not everyone follows the same religion and that's okay. It's called the First Amendment. One of the great things about America is we have the freedom to practice whatever religion we want or to not practice any religion at all. So here's a newsflash to you, the jackass. If someone says or writes any of the following,

Happy Holidays

Feliz Navidad

Happy Hannukkah

Joyous Kwanzaa

Merry Xmas

Merry Christmas

Season's Greetings

Don't be a jackass and try to "correct" them or get angry because they didn't greet you in the manner of your own religious beliefs. According to the Pew Research Center (2013)[xv], 81% of non-Christians in the U.S. celebrate Christmas. This includes people of no particular faith as well as people of other faiths. Whether you view Christmastime as a religious holiday or as a cultural event, be gracious in accepting another person's seasonal greetings. Our cultural landscape grows more diverse by the day. America is supposed to be the land of acceptance and tolerance. That person sending you their greeting might be a Christian, but they very well could be agnostic, atheist, Buddhist, Hindu, Jewish, or Muslim.

If your response to a greeting from someone whose only goal is to endear themselves to you is a negative one, then you're a jackass. End of story.

8 CONCLUSION

Just as the human race continues to evolve, so too does our ability to communicate. The means by which we communicate have expanded and changed, as well—from leaving marks on cave walls to leaving comments on virtual walls. It's important to note how easy it is for us to forget regardless of the means we use to communicate, there is another human being at the receiving end of the message. We have a responsibility to be mindful of how our messages may positively or negatively impact other people and how those messages impact others' perceptions of us. To act otherwise is just plain idiotic.

Remember this:

- *Talk less, listen more, and listen correctly.*

- *Upgrade to the Golden Rule 2.0.*

- *Quit blaming others; look first in the mirror for change.*

- *Practice mindful communication; create a shared meaning.*

- *Technology isn't an invisibility cloak; it's a permanent record.*

- *What you're saying might be legal, but is it responsible?*

- *Say please, thank you, and you're welcome.*

- *Respect is a reflection of your character, not theirs.*

Now, that's not so hard is it?

I hope this book helps improve your communication skills, which will, in turn, lead to healthier and more fulfilling personal and professional relationships. Whether it's about the talking, or the listening, or the writing, we can all use some help in figuring out how to be better communicators.

There are already too many jackasses in this world. We run across them every single day. When you look in the mirror, make sure there's not a jackass looking back.

ABOUT THE AUTHOR

Jennifer Arvin Furlong was born and raised in Augusta, Georgia. At the age of 18 she joined the U.S. Marine Corps where she became the first woman Marine to serve as editor for the Quantico Sentry newspaper and to be awarded the Sergeant Major Dan Daly Award. She was also awarded Best Feature Writer by the Marine Corps Combat Correspondents Association. After the Corps, Furlong worked in the communication industry and mainly focused on community relations, writing, and editing. She earned a B.A and M.A. in Communication from George Mason University. She stumbled into her second career in higher education during her graduate program due to a chance teaching opportunity and has been torturing college students in human communication and public speaking ever since. She is currently studying for her Ph.D. in English Language and Applied Linguistics with the University of Birmingham – UK.

i COMMUNICATION. (2015). RETRIEVED FROM GOOGLE HTTPS://WWW.GOOGLE.COM/WEBHP?SOURCE=SEARCH_APP#Q=DEFINITION+OF+COMMUNICATION

ii BY PERMISSION. FROM MERRIAM-WEBSTER'S COLLEGIATE® DICTIONARY, 11TH EDITION ©2016 BY MERRIAM-WEBSTER, INC. (HTTP://WWW.MERRIAM-WEBSTER.COM/DICTIONARY/COMMUNICATION).

iii COMMUNICATION. (2015). RETRIEVED FROM THE ENCYCLOPEDIA BRITANNICA HTTP://WWW.BRITANNICA.COM/EBCHECKED/TOPIC/129024/COMMUNICATION

iv BY PERMISSION. FROM MERRIAM-WEBSTER'S COLLEGIATE® DICTIONARY, 11TH EDITION ©2016 BY MERRIAM-WEBSTER, INC. HTTP://WWW.MERRIAM-WEBSTER.COM/DICTIONARY/GOLDEN%20RULE

v HUMANITY HEALING INTERNATIONAL, INC. THE GOLDEN RULE. N.D. WEB. 14 JULY 2016

vi LARRY KING. (N.D.). BRAINYQUOTE.COM. RETRIEVED JULY 27, 2016, FROM BRAINYQUOTE.COM WEB SITE: HTTP://WWW.BRAINYQUOTE.COM/QUOTES/AUTHORS/L/LARRY_KING.HTML

vii SOCIAL NETWORKING FACT SHEET. (2013). PEW RESEARCH CENTER: INTERNET, SCIENCE & TECH. RETRIEVED FROM HTTP://WWW.PEWINTERNET.ORG/FACT-SHEETS/SOCIAL-NETWORKING-FACT-SHEET/

viii FACEBOOK REPORTS SECOND QUARTER 2016 RESULTS. (2016). RETRIEVED FROM HTTP://INVESTOR.FB.COM/RELEASEDETAIL.CFM?RELEASEID=780093

ix TWITTER. (2016, JUNE). TWITTER USAGE / COMPANY FACTS. RETRIEVED FROM TWITTER WEBSITE HTTPS://ABOUT.TWITTER.COM/COMPANY

x ON DEVICE RESEARCH. (2013, MAY 29). IMPACT OF SOCIAL MEDIA ON CAREERS. [WEB LOG]. FACEBOOK COSTING 16-34S JOBS IN TOUGH ECONOMIC CLIMATE. RETRIEVED FROM HTTPS://ONDEVICERESEARCH.COM/BLOG/FACEBOOK-COSTING-16-34S-JOBS-IN-TOUGH-ECONOMIC-CLIMATE

xi THE U.S. NATIONAL ARCHIVES AND RECORDS ADMINISTRATION. (2016, AUGUST). BILL OF RIGHTS. RETRIEVED FROM US NARA WEBSITE HTTP://WWW.ARCHIVES.GOV/EXHIBITS/CHARTERS/BILL_OF_RIGHTS_TRANSCRIPT.HTML

xii The Administrative Office of the U.S. Courts. (2016, August). What does free speech mean? Retrieved from US Courts website http://www.uscourts.gov/educational-resources/get-involved/constitution-activities/first-amendment/free-speech.aspx

xiii Hudson, D. (2002, September). Pledge of allegiance. Newseuminstitute. Retrieved from http://www.newseuminstitute.org/pledge-of-allegiance/

xiv Calvert, C. (2014, July). Telling the police to f*** off: Risky first amendment business. Newseuminstitute. Retrieved from http://www.newseuminstitute.org/telling-the-police-to-f-off-risky-first-amendment-business/

xv Mohamed, B. (2013). Christmas also celebrated by many non-Christians. PewResearchCenter. Retrieved from http://www.pewresearch.org/fact-tank/2013/12/23/christmas-also-celebrated-by-many-non-christians/

Figure 1
VanLoon, K. and McKenna, P. (2000). The golden rule. Retrieved from http://www.scarboromissions.ca/wp-content/uploads/2015/01/item_34_lg.jpg

Coming Soon!

Mini-Handbook for Jackasses: Interviewing & Workplace Communication

Mini-Handbook for Jackasses: Public Speaking

Mini-Handbook for Jackasses: Going to College

www.ingramcontent.com/pod-product-compliance
Lightning Source LLC
Chambersburg PA
CBHW041217270326
41931CB00001B/4